THE FLYING PINEAPPLE

Jamie Baulch

SHORTLIST

First published in 2011 by
Accent Press Ltd
This Large Print edition published
2011 by AudioGO Ltd
by arrangement with
Accent Press Ltd

ISBN 978 1 4056 2315 5

British Library Cataloguing in Publication Data available

Printed and bound in Great Britain
by MPG Books Group Limited

INTRODUCTION

My family mean everything to me. I can honestly say that I am happiest when I am surrounded by my parents, Alan and Marilyn, my brother and sisters David, Lucy and Sarah, my partner Susannah and my sons, Jay and Morgan. They are more important to me than all the medals I have won in athletics.

It's been said that I am one of the most decorated British athletes. That's because in my career I've been part of the British relay teams and competed in the Indoor Championships as well as the individual 400 metres events. I've got an Olympic silver medal, European gold, World gold, silver and bronze, Commonwealth bronze . . . the list goes on. Of more value to me, though, above all these, is my family.

When I look back on my career,

it is because of them that I feel as successful as I am told I have been. They have always been there for me. I shared the early joy of winning races with my parents and siblings. Now I can look back on what I have achieved and know I am as proud of my sons as my parents were of me. I knew they always believed in me and I try to make sure my sons feel the same way. I follow their acting and performance successes, looking on from the sidelines exactly as my dad did for me. My parents always made us feel that they were proud of us all, no matter what we achieved or to what level. I want my sons to grow up feeling that way too.

CHAPTER ONE

HAPPY FAMILIES

I have two sisters and one brother and I am the baby of the family.

Two of us were adopted—Sarah, my older sister, and me. I was three months old when I was adopted by my mum and dad in 1973. I'm of mixed race but I grew up in a white family. My dad is an architect and my mum a school teacher in Cwmbrân. Growing up in south Wales in the 70s, people would say, 'You look like your dad,' though I looked nothing like him. We still laugh about that. We were, and are, a very loving family. I give full credit to my mum and dad that I don't remember anything but a happy childhood and home life. To this day, Mum and Dad's home is central to all of us. Whenever I chat to anyone else about their upbringing they always say that I'm really lucky, and I feel it.

My parents live in a farmhouse with six acres of land, so as children we had fields all around us and a big front garden where we played. When I was growing up, we used to go down to the south of France once a year in the summer holidays, caravanning. It was perfect and we all loved being together as a family. Christmas time for us has always been a real community and family time. We always got the presents we asked for and, far more importantly, the love and attention. We weren't spoilt but, if I'm honest, out of the four of us, I think I was the most spoilt because I was the baby. I was the one who always got away with murder, and I became a cheeky chap, because I was allowed to get away with it! My parents said that when I used to come into the living room, I could never sit quietly on the settee. I'd come from behind it, dive to tumble in a forward roll and land loudly and forcefully. I was always raring to go and always active.

I'm sure one of the reasons I've got to where I am today is because of the support I had growing up. Mine were never pushy parents, but they were always there when we needed them. I played football for the Under Tens and my dad was the sponge man who used to run on every time somebody got injured. He was the sponge man when I played cricket in Croesyceiliog, too, so he was always there on hand and enjoyed being part of the team. As a child, I'd always have the right kit and Mum and Dad worked hard to give us the best. They raised the four of us exactly alike. They worked very hard and are extremely humble, and I am proud of how they brought us up. It's rubbed off on me and, through me, on to my children.

Even now, at the age of thirty-seven, if I am in doubt about something or I need advice, I'll still ring up my parents and talk it through with them. No matter what the problem, I go to them and they are there for me, as they always have been. I feel very fortunate that the relationship we have is like that. I never had any problems with adolescence. Maybe that's just the way I am but I was never an angry teenager—I've always loved life.

We were a sporty family. My brother played badminton and both my sisters played county tennis, and were very good players. My older sister also played hockey. But I was the only runner. Dad played cricket a lot when he was younger. When we went to France each year, we all played tennis, went swimming and played table tennis. Every year I used to run against my dad on the beach over 50 metres. One year I flew past him and beat him by about 10 metres. I left him standing and he's never raced me since! It was a big moment in my life, to beat my dad. As if I'd suddenly become a man myself. I had just beaten the man who was, and would always be, a hero to me. All through my childhood I looked up to my dad and I still do, but to beat him then was very special.

We're a very competitive family and that meant that board games were always interesting! Whenever we played Monopoly, whoever was the banker would always win as money wouldn't stay in the bank! We used to fight and argue over the game when we were in our caravan, so the French neighbours must have wondered what the noise was in the evenings.

As a family we are all very proud of each other and what we have achieved. All of us children have done well. My brother is a surveyor, my sister is a teacher in Dubai and my other sister has worked on a private yacht. We're a very international family, too. I'm obviously used to travelling the world to compete in athletics, but my sisters have also found success abroad. Thanks to Mum and Dad, we have international tastes in food, as we were brought up to try out food from different countries. I've followed this tradition with my children and they aren't afraid to try any foods abroad.

People have asked whether I have ever wanted to trace my birth family. I say that my mum and dad are my mum and dad. I've never been interested in finding anyone else. My mum has been my mum as long as I have been aware, as I was hers from the age of three months. I know I was born in Nottingham, which is difficult for me as a very patriotic Welshman! And I know my dad was Jamaican and my mum was British. But I've never wanted to look beyond the wonderful family I have, because they are the only family I've known and they have given me the most amazing life. We don't look like each other, but they love me and I love them. They brought me up and they are my mum and dad. Why would I look for anything else? What would I be looking for? I've got all the answers I need. I have all the love and care of parents who chose to have me. I couldn't have been luckier.

As I have grown older, I think of my biological mum as someone who had to make a tough decision to have me, when she could have chosen not to, and I am thankful she made that choice. For me that's where it starts and finishes.

CHAPTER TWO

FINDING MY FEET

When I look back at my sporting schooldays, I was one of the best in school and I always really enjoyed taking part, but I was never *the* best. However, in athletics, from a young age, in running terms, I was pretty good. When I was about nine or ten years old, I was so much faster than everyone in my year. I could go up to the next year group to compete and still beat them, which doesn't happen often in schools, because at that age children get so much bigger and stronger in a year. I remember the day it all started to happen for me. It was a Sports Day in Henllys School, Cwmbrân, and I was ten years old and really enjoying myself doing an event called the obstacle race. You had to run with an egg and spoon for

10

ten metres, go over a long wooden bench for another five metres, then get in a sack and jump in the sack for ten metres. Finally, you had to go underneath a mattress before sprinting for the finish. The race started and everyone was cheering. I set off running with the egg and spoon, went over the bench, jumped into the sack, went underneath the mattress and I ended up coming out at the side, not at the front as I was supposed to. The headmaster stuck firmly, and rightly, to the rules, and said, 'You've got to go back to the start, Jamie.' So I went all the way back to the start, picked up the egg and spoon, went over the bench, jumped into the sack, went underneath the mattress, sprinted to the finish and won the race! I was twice as fast as the others, and that's when I really believe I started my athletics! I remember being determined to catch up and win, so I did. I wanted to be the fastest and I wanted to win.

Luckily for me, my headmaster, Mr Atkins, was a runner from Newport and he trained with Newport Harriers. He convinced me that I had a talent and suggested I join a club. So the following week, I went down with my mum and my granddad on a Tuesday night to the club to enrol. Even though I was young, I knew that this was something I really wanted to do. I trained that night, and I trained again on the following Thursday, as I could feel it was good for me. And, about a month later, I entered the local county championships and won the 100 metres.

I was lucky enough to have a head teacher who believed in the power of sport and who wanted to help me achieve. He took the time and effort to encourage me. I played lots of different sports—tennis, football, cricket—but athletics was my passion.

Mr Atkins was a really positive influence on me. I would see him at the running club and he would ask me how my running was getting on. As a young boy, I felt quite cool seeing my headmaster outside school. He showed an interest in my running and asked about my progress, and I felt proud that I was doing what he had asked me to try. There was a social aspect to the sport too, and that was exciting.

All my teachers became an important influence when they could see my talent. Mr Knight and Mr Hopkins taught PE in my secondary school, Risca Comprehensive, and would stay behind after school and coach me. I really appreciate how much of their time they gave to after-school clubs and teams. That to me is real dedication and I'm sure other pupils in my school feel the same way. School for me was a very happy time. My favourite subject was obviously PE but I also really enjoyed Art and Graphics. I didn't really like English or Mathematics, as I'm a more visual person, but I was quite good at Art. I remember drawing a picture in my Art class where half my face was my own and half was the face of a devil. In the background I drew a running track. The picture showed how I felt during the pain of training, how hard you had to work and that the devil comes out in you to get you to the finish line. I was very pleased with it and the teacher understood and could see what I was trying to show. My school reports always said the same thing: that I was happy and enthusiastic, or I was friendly and sociable, but the last line always said I needed to concentrate more. I think that's probably fair.

School was fun for me. I had lots of friends and I was a happy-go-lucky pupil. I was never alone, always had a lot of energy, and never liked sitting down too long. My favourite school day was always Sports Day. It was a day I could shine and I took part in as many events as I could.

However, probably one of the worst moments in my athletic career happened during one of my Sports Days. The whole school was watching as I competed in the long jump. I was really pleased that I could do the hitch kick like one of my heroes, Carl Lewis. I ran down the runway, jumped in the air, did a hitch kick and landed much further forward than anyone else. As I landed, though, I broke wind loudly. The crowd was silent until someone shouted loudly, 'That was Baulchy!' I was so embarrassed. But the only way to deal with it was to throw my hands in the air, admit it and laugh at myself.

I was part of a very happy, positive group of people and I'm still best friends with people I was at school with. I'm very proud that we are still friends after all these years. Some of my friends I met playing Under Tens football and that shows the strength of our friendship. Matt Wintle, Chris Williams and Nick Pritchard are three friends who are very important to me. I first met Nick Pritchard on the school bus which took us all to Risca School. Nick was much bigger than me at the time. He turned around to me on the bus and, looking tough, said, 'Where are you from, butt?' I wouldn't back down and said, 'Cwmbrân, butt.' 'So what do you do?' he said, and I announced, 'I'm a runner.' We still laugh about that first meeting now. We did race. I won. But we're still best mates to this day.

CHAPTER THREE

BE YOURSELF

After Risca Comprehensive, I enrolled at Pontypool College to do a PE Foundation course. My tutors there, Avril Williams and Phil Jones, were as supportive as my school teachers had been. Avril Williams was very keen on athletics and she used to judge at Welsh national level. In Pontypool College, I took part in the full range of sports, even trampolining, where I came second in the 1991 Welsh Schools Championships. The tutors made sure that we all did a lot of very different sports to work on our different strengths and weaknesses so that we raised our fitness levels quickly. My running really improved and I managed to beat Colin Jackson's Welsh record at

200 metres. I improved so much because of the encouragement I received from the lecturers, and being around other talented people made us all improve. By trying so many different sports we met the best in each of them and that made us raise our game to try to be as good.

My mum and dad, again, were equally supportive. They used to take me everywhere around Britain to train and compete. It was nothing for them to drive me to Exeter, Sheffield or Gateshead. Most of the time it was just the three of us in the car but sometimes the rest of the family would come to watch as well. Dad would blast the stereo and the track I remember him playing a lot was Gabrielle's 'Dreams'. The song says 'Dreams can come true' and I loved hearing it. There are two songs that mean a lot to my dad and me: that one, and 'Barcelona'. Sometimes, Dad would play 'Barcelona' at full blast in the house while Mum laughed. He wanted me to do well and was passionate for me. I never felt any pressure from them to do well, but I just understood how much I meant to them and how much they wanted the very best for me.

When I was in my early teens and up to the age of sixteen, my parents found a good way to get me to achieve in my races. When I started doing well, becoming best in the county and moving up to one of the best in Wales, my dad would tell me that if I ran well, they would take me to a steak house after the race. At the time, I thought that was the best prize ever—so I ran for steak! We still laugh about it now. I would run as fast as I could, win the race and then Mum and Dad would take me for steak and chips at a Berni Inn steak house. I used to love it.

When I got even better, my aunties and uncles joined in with incentives. I was at the British Junior

Championships in Stoke at the age of seventeen and my auntie and uncle, Mike and Coral Dark, said that if I ran well they would buy me a tracksuit. I ran really well and came second in the British Championships. I was only seventeen, so I was the youngest in the race. And it was Darren Campbell, an excellent British running talent, who beat me, so although I wasn't first, I was beaten by a champion. My auntie and uncle kept their word and bought me the tracksuit I really wanted. It was very expensive for the time and cost £99. It was a silver Gore-Tex shell suit, like a space outfit. It was really cool and I wish I still had it! I loved wearing it. I looked like an astronaut in it. I was always different to the other competitors then and I think I still am. As an athlete, I never liked to look the same as everyone else. I didn't do it to be difficult but it's just my personality.

My hair was always important to

me. As a kid, I used to have a flat-top like Kid 'n Play and Carl Lewis, short on the sides and flat on top. In college, I got bored with this and felt it was time for a change, so I braided my hair to look like Jazzy B and Soul II Soul. It took six hours for the hairdresser to finish the job, which meant I got to watch *Neighbours* at lunchtime and again in the evening repeat! Then I prepared myself for the grand unveiling to my mum. I remember thinking she would kill me. I opened the front door slowly, walked into the living room and there she was waiting for me to come home.

She looked at me for a few seconds before smiling and telling me how much she liked my new hairstyle. That was it! If my mum didn't mind me having crazy hair I had a whole new way to express myself! After this, I tied the braids up and they looked just like a pineapple on my head. Later in my career, when I bleached the braids, was when my nickname of the Flying Pineapple was born.

My dress sense got me noticed, too. I had my Converse boots to warm up on the track, which wasn't what the other athletes wore. They wore trainers but I was proud of my boots and my spaceman's outfit. A month later in Salamanca, Spain, at an athletics meet, I was told off by the British team manager for wearing the boots. He said loudly, 'What are those on your feet?' I replied, 'They're boots, sir.' He was disgusted and snapped, 'They're not running shoes, Baulch.' Cheekily I laughed and said, 'Yeah, but I feel cool in these, sir.' I ended up winning and also breaking the Welsh record. People said, 'Who is this guy?' but then I'd win or at least I'd be up there in the top three. Even when we went out after training, I didn't want to look like the others. I borrowed my sister Sarah's tartan baggy trousers and teamed them with a suit jacket and chunky black shoes. I thought that I looked stylish. I took the criticism from my mates who laughed at me constantly and it definitely got me a lot of attention. But my running was what got me noticed most of all.

Around this time, I remember Darren Campbell, who was then the best in Great Britain and one of the best in the world at 100 metres and 200 metres, saying to me when we had a quiet moment that I was different to the others as I didn't copy him. He noticed that all the other competitors copied him because he was the best. I replied, 'Why would I want to follow you?' He appreciated that I was my own person and it made our friendship all the more strong. He could see the independence in me. I wanted to be my own master. I always recognised how good or how talented other people were but I wanted to be myself. I put that down to my family and my upbringing.

CHAPTER FOUR

GETTING SERIOUS

When I first started training seriously I used to watch Colin Jackson train at Cwmbrân stadium with the hurdler Nigel Walker. Sometimes I would also see Linford Christie there with them. They were some of the fastest men on the planet and I wanted to make it like them. Just seeing them train made me want to achieve their successes. I used to watch them in the weights room laughing and giggling and I really wanted to be one of their group.

Linford didn't come regularly but, when he did, he made a big impression as the athlete from London who wasn't one of our local heroes. I remember him sitting once in the stand at Cwmbrân Stadium with hardly anyone around him. I went up to him with a group of young athletes and asked him what times he had run when he was fifteen years old. He took time to talk to me, I was thrilled that my times were close to his. It was very important to me that the great Linford Christie had talked to me. Years later, I became one of his training group and finally achieved my ambition to be one of them.

People ask me when I knew I was going to make it as an athlete. I think it was racing against Colin Jackson at the age of seventeen in Cardiff stadium. I had made it to the final of the 100 metres race and, feeling that I had made it just by being in the same race as such a star, I started fooling about on the start line in my usual way. Colin turned to me and said firmly, 'Jamie, concentrate.' I remember being suddenly still and thinking that being told this by someone like Colin meant I needed to take it seriously. I immediately stopped fooling about and switched myself on, taking the advice of a great sportsman who had wanted me to give my best. I suddenly understood that I could no longer mess about. They say that in every athlete's life there is a defining moment and this was mine. Colin beat me—but only just. I crossed the line and thought to myself that even though this wasn't Colin's event he was a very good sprinter, so that coming close to him really meant something.

That incident was a defining moment in more ways than one. Colin Jackson was a legend and, to him, it was just another race but he took time to tell me to focus and make the effort that I needed. I was awed that he had spoken to me and it pulled me up sharply and made me so much better. This was a man who I had watched on the television and who I had looked up to since the start of my career.

He had told me to concentrate as a matter of urgency and when I was told by him, I listened. I ran 10.77 seconds and I had never run under 11 seconds before that day. It was a huge achievement and it meant a lot to me. I was delighted to be on the same rostrum as Colin and in all the pictures I was beaming with delight.

The next week, I opened *Athletics Weekly* magazine sure that my name would be there and excited that people would now know who I was. I flicked through excitedly looking everywhere to see my name and finally, right at the back of the magazine, found the piece on the Welsh Championships. It said, 'First—Colin Jackson. Second—James Beluchi.' I was furious that they had got my name wrong and I hadn't got the piece I had hoped for. Typical, I thought. A few weeks later, at the British Championships, I came third behind Darren Campbell and still they got my name wrong! It was only the following day, coming around the bend in the 200 metres, that I heard the magical announcement, 'In the patriotic colours of Wales we have James Baulch.' Finally, I had made it!

My running was going well and I came first in the 1992 World Junior Championships in the 4 × 100 metres relay where we broke the World Junior record. The team consisted of Allyn Condon, now a British bobsleigh champion, Darren Campbell on second leg, myself on third leg and Jason Fergus, now a well-known coach, on the final leg. While we were waiting to race, the American team had tried to rile us by jeering that we couldn't win as our team had a white runner in the squad. It all got quite heated and going out to race we felt we had something to prove. But we won, and, standing to collect our medals, Allyn Condon turned to the Americans and grinned before saying, 'Not bad for a white guy!' We were a team regardless of colour. For us, it was about being the fastest and we proved we were.

At that time, I ran 100 metres and 200 metres races alongside really great 200 metres runners like Darren Campbell and Ato Boldon. This showed that I was getting much better as I was holding my own in the races. The move from Junior to Senior level is a hard step—you move into races where you compete against the very best. At this point, I was very lucky: Colin Jackson saw something in me and offered to coach me after the Commonwealth Games. Who would argue with an offer like that? It was a great chance and I took it.

I had been with my old coach Jim Anderson, or Jock as he is known, for some time. He was an excellent coach who had looked after some great athletes but I felt it was time to move on. Jock had been a wonderful influence in my life. He looked and talked like Rab C Nesbitt and it took me about two years to understand what he was saying when he coached me! But he was a very special coach to me and, despite his swearing, I realised that he thought a great deal of me and wanted the best for me. He was a traditional coach and believed in 'old school' regimented methods. We used to train using the speedball which is what boxers do, like in the *Rocky* films. Jock's training group included Christian Malcolm and I knew he would one day become an international athlete even at that stage. Jock and my dad used to love spending time together. One thing I do remember is that having driven all the way to Horsham to watch me run they missed my race because they were both in the bar together. It took them some time to live that down!

But Colin was an amazing mentor

and coach and I owe him greatly. He wrote in his biography that 'Coaching Jamie Baulch was one of the brightest sparks in my life.' I have to say that he helped light up my career. I had no money at this point and Colin paid for me so that I could continue as an athlete. As a senior, I hadn't won any medals and so I had no cash. I joined Colin's training group in America where we lived as a team and Colin supervised our training. To have Colin Jackson offer to coach me was inspirational. The house in Florida had a pool and my dream was to relax there next to it with the sun beating down. That wasn't to be. The reality was that Colin was such a success because he was so focused and committed. We had times to train, to eat and to sleep. It was disciplined and we had to commit. But it worked, and Colin knew how to make us all more successful. He was proof of that himself.

Colin watched our diets, our training plans and a year later I won an Olympic silver medal. It was worth being refused sweets! Colin always kept a sweet jar in the kitchen and it was full of my favourite jelly sweets. It was taped at the top and he wrote his name across it to ensure that we couldn't eat them without him noticing. I used to go shopping and then hide sweets I had bought in my pillow or around the room. One day Colin asked me if I had been eating sweets and I denied it. He suggested I look in the mirror. There, to my shame, was a chocolate perfectly stuck to the side of my mouth as I had tried to cram it in without him catching me!

Today we laugh together about his house rules. But then, there was a time to work and a time to mess about. We all had chores to do in the house and he made sure it was spotless. He always prided himself on doing a job properly. We used to have Sundays off from the training track and I looked forward to a lie-in when I could. One Sunday morning, I could hear the vacuum cleaner getting louder and louder until eventually it was bumping on the bedroom door. I was furious but I was so sleepy that I didn't want to get up. Finally I couldn't stand the noise any more. I got out of bed and threw open the door to find the vacuum cleaner had been left there, plugged in, and it was bashing against the door. Colin was the other side of the house watching television and laughing at the trick he'd played on me.

He was strict but fair and, if we wanted to be the best, we knew he could make us winners. I suddenly had to grow up. Colin liked to have fun but he worked hard and was totally serious about his training and set himself clear goals. I'm a very different character because I'm more happy-go-lucky. So he taught me a great deal. Today I call him my lottery grant. His time and money helped me to succeed.

Colin's regime worked and I ran 44.57 seconds at my new distance of 400 metres. He had made me so fit that when I took on 400 metres races, I broke the Welsh record and even Colin was in shock! I was suddenly ranked second in Britain at a time when there were great 400 metres runners around, like Mark Richardson, Iwan Thomas and Roger Black. I had found my distance and, thanks to Colin, had found my speed. It was special to be coached by Colin, Colin the legend but also a fellow Welshman. We are from the same area in south Wales and both of us are proud to represent Wales.

CHAPTER FIVE

DO IT FOR THE KIDS

Pontypool College was the place where I started to achieve real sporting results but, far more importantly to me, it was the place where I met my girlfriend, Susannah. I was seventeen. She was doing a drama course and I remember seeing her and thinking how attractive she was. I was going out with another girl at the time but Susannah and I started chatting by the vending machine in college and later that day she sat next to my girlfriend in her English class and my girlfriend confided to her that she was worried that I was interested in somebody else. The rest is history.

Although breaking the Welsh record was a high point for me, an even more important moment in my life was about to happen. In May 1995, my son Jay was born. I was called from the rugby club where I was out with my dad and I drove madly to the hospital to be there at the birth. From the moment of seeing my son, I was in love with him. The bond between us was instant. He was me, in looks and mannerisms.

For me, being a dad was absolutely wonderful. Susannah and I were young parents but very responsible and both of us wanted the best for our new family. My world changed with the arrival of my son. I wanted to be as good to him as my parents had been to me. I knew that the key to giving my son and my girlfriend the best was for me to raise my game, and I trained hard to make this happen. My son had to have the same benefits my parents had worked so hard to give me. I loved being a dad and cleaned bottles and changed nappies. Our flat was small but we were a very happy family and my running improved with my new motivation. In the words of one of my heroes, Lynn Davies, a Welsh sporting legend and long jump Olympic gold medallist, 'It's not about commitment. It's about total commitment.' I had to train hard and win races and commit to making myself a champion. I had to grow up and I wanted to achieve for my son.

It was around this time that I was racing in Australia and the commentator, Maurie Plant, a well-known and much-respected figure in athletics, announced the lane draw. When he came to me, he said, 'In lane five, Jamie Baulch—the flying pineapple!' My nickname was born.

Darren Campbell and I were best mates, in track and field terms, and in life. When we went to the European Championships, the World Championships and the Olympics, we'd always share a room. We are both proud fathers who want the best for our children and we have an expression 'Do it for the kids'. Whenever we were on our last legs in training, however sick we felt, that's what we said. We understood that if we didn't put the extra in, one of our competitors always would. I wasn't the most naturally talented athlete but I was one of the ones who trained the hardest and that's what paid off for me.

It wasn't all work though as I had a good group of friends—Darren Campbell, Matt Elias the 400 metres Welsh sprinter, Katherine Merry the 400 metres Olympic bronze medallist, Paul Gray the 110 metres hurdler and Commonwealth Games bronze medallist . . . all well known in athletics but all mates to me.

We worked hard, but played hard too. At the 1997 World Championships in Athens, David Dix was in charge of the British kit. He went for lunch one day and Darren and I decided to go to his room and hide all the British kit.

We took it back to our room and hid it in the toilet, locked our door and went off for the day. Dix was a mild-mannered man but he went completely wild, thinking that the kit had been taken by one of the other teams. We told him several hours later and although he was relieved, we left quickly before he made us pay for our actions.

Darren and I were the jokers in the team and although our characters were very different, we got on well. I was the happy, funny one and Darren was known for being tough, with a cool swagger, but together we had a great laugh. John Regis, the Great Britain sprinter, was sent to our room to film a piece about the teams. He asked each of us what was annoying about the other as roommates. I jumped in saying how much it irritated me that Darren went to sleep at night leaving the television on. It infuriated me that he needed it on to sleep and kept the controls with him and I wasn't able to sleep with the noise. I couldn't think what might be irritating about me to him, of course! He looked at me scornfully and said that after every shower, I threw my wet towel on his bed. I had no idea I was driving him mad—and that put me in my place! We still meet up now and talk about the good old times together.

He and I were also the jokers at the 1996 Olympics in Atlanta. Golf buggies were used by officials to transport athletes to and from the track. One night, Darren decided to 'borrow' one for us. He hotwired the buggy, laughing to me, 'It's because I'm from Manchester that I know how to do this!' He managed to start the buggy with a drinks can ring-pull and we drove around the athletes' village in our golf buggy like the Dukes of Hazzard. Unfortunately, Darren's driving wasn't as good as his hotwiring skills and we ended up crashing down an embankment and hitting the British team management's office window. That was when we really put our British sprinting skills to good use, to get away quickly from the scene of the crime.

I loved my first Olympic Games. We were given our British team kit— everything from clothes to shoes to sunglasses. I remember being so excited and rushing to put it on and parade around in my parents' front garden and have photographs taken. Getting the letter through our front door saying that I had been invited to represent Great Britain in the 4×400 metres relay was an amazing moment. I was so proud of achieving that, and going to the Olympic Games in America would be a dream come true. I was in the best shape of my life and I was proud to be part of the relay team but understood that because of the massive strength in British 400 metres running at the time, it would be a tough fight to get a place in the individual event. Four British athletes had run under 45 seconds at the British trials. I wasn't bitter that I didn't get chosen as I had done the best I could have done. Roger Black had broken the British record. The crowd went wild and I went home smiling from the trials, having played my part in an outstanding sporting moment for athletics.

When we arrived in Atlanta, I shared a room with Darren Campbell and we were in bunk beds, he on the bottom bed and me on the top. We had a little CD player with small speakers and stayed up listening to Keith Sweat. Darren and I quickly found the games room at the village and used to play on the machines there as we weren't allowed out of the Olympic Village. Two days before my race we were there playing Quasar, enjoying ourselves very noisily, and a huge American security guard came in and asked us to leave. When we asked why, we were told the Vice President of the United States was coming in to the games room to play Quasar. We never did find out if that was true!

Before the relay, I sat with Iwan Thomas, Mark Richardson, Mark Hilton, Roger Black and Du'aine Ladejo and we talked about how we could win. There were six of us in the relay team and we were told that those who ran the fastest leg of the relay in the heats would be the four chosen for the final. It was hard to hear that, but it was the only way to decide who would have to be left out. We needed to talk to each other to make the team work, but it felt horrible to know that two of us would not be in the final team. There was a real feeling of fear around us. My stomach was churning when I realised it was time for the final decision. It was between Du'aine and myself, as Roger Black had secured his place by gaining a silver medal in the Olympics at 400 metres. Iwan and Mark Richardson had also done well and gained their places in the team. But in the heats I ran a second faster than Du'aine and got my place in the final. I was so relieved, but upset for Du'aine too, as I knew how he must have felt, being left out.

As individuals, we were all very different people but together we made a great team. Iwan and I were the characters in the team. Mark Richardson was an incredibly nice, very well-mannered man and Roger Black was the people's favourite, with a string of medals already. Two Welshmen and two Englishmen on one team made for an interesting combination but one that worked. By now, my blond dreadlocks were very well known and, around this time, I won the BBC Radio 1 hairstyle of the year, beating David Beckham! Roger Black was the darling of the mums but I had the younger vote.

Putting a winning relay team

together is hard. As well as the talent for running the individual legs, you also have to have belief in your team-mates. We were all very different, but together we were a very strong force. Our personalities complimented each other. And we all had respect for each other. Before the final, we went as a team to McDonald's in the Olympic village and had chicken nuggets and chips and were given our team brief. Looking back on it now, it is strange to think that that was our meal before running such an important race! We all wore the Great Britain training kit as we wanted to look like a team. It was decided Iwan would run the first leg, as he always ran a great and consistent opening, and would get us into a good position. I was to run the second leg because I could change gear and accelerate sharply. Mark Richardson was the reliable third man who was beautiful to watch as a runner and a superb part of a relay team. Finally, Roger was given the home straight, battling to the last.

We all boarded the bus with our athletes' passes around our neck. Security was really tight and without these passes it didn't matter who you were, you wouldn't get into the Olympic stadium. The tension was building.

In the final, we were up against the American team. They were a seriously powerful team, and it really was a classic finale for an Olympic Games. I can remember feeling the atmosphere in the stadium as we prepared to do battle, and it sent a shiver down my spine. This was my one shot. I had to get it right on the day, at that hour, at that minute. I had to present myself, perform at my best and deliver. I looked around the huge stadium taking in the size of the crowd and realising exactly what was about to happen. As a team, we were like warriors, looking into each other's eyes, pumping each other up with powerful words. It was controlled aggression. None of us wanted to let our team-mates down. This was what we had prepared for during all those hard training sessions. I felt loose and light and as the gun went off, signalling Iwan had started, I thought to myself: this is my time.

As soon as I started running, all the fear, the anxiety and the tension drained away. It was me in my lane on that track and it was me against the others and against the clock. I was running against one of the two Harrison brothers. I got the baton from Iwan and I remember feeling very alive. All my senses were heightened and I was scared, but totally excited. I could feel the sweat on my body and it was as if I was only aware of myself and no one else at all in a stadium of thousands of people. I knew I was in great shape for the race and I said to myself,

'It's the final. Let's do it!' As I raced around the bend, the American Alvin Harrison drew next to me and said scornfully, 'Oh yeah baby!' I was furious that he thought I couldn't react. He was ahead but I dug in, ran straight past him and as I did, made the 'Meep, Meep' noises like Roadrunner!

In the end the Americans got the gold and we won the silver, as they were the better team on the day. It would have been good to have beaten them but we were realistic. Together, the four of us did a lap of honour, waving to the crowd, holding the British flag high in the air. Cameras were flashing and people were screaming from the crowd and from the British team stand. The American team had won the prize, but I always felt that I had won my own battle out there on the track that day.

CHAPTER SIX

ON MY OWN

Winning the silver medal at my first Olympic Games was a huge achievement for me. Our team still holds the European and Commonwealth record for the 4 × 400 metres relay even now. I was training with Colin Jackson and mixing with all of the great athletes at the time, like Linford Christie and the decathlete Daley Thompson, so I was really learning from the best. I was one of a successful group of athletes who were recognised wherever we went, and life was fun.

I was winning all of my races and I felt on top of the world. I knew I was strong and my confidence seemed to affect those I raced against— they were worried by me. When I entered races my opponents saw me as favourite and that made them more nervous. I was even asked on American television to speak about the great Michael Johnson, and asked if I thought I could take him on. I'm sure he would have beaten me but I was proud that they had suggested I had a chance against such a champion. I was a clear favourite in the Indoors races and looked forward to the World Indoor Championships in Paris that year. All my family, my parents, Susannah and Jay, my sister, aunts and uncles came to watch me in Paris, expecting a big success. Even a school friend, Dean Harris from Risca Comprehensive, flew to Paris just for the event.

Sadly, it was not to be a success for me. I hate to talk about it even now. I got to the final of the competition but my inexperience in handling the pressure of a World Championships individual final got to me. I was rooming with Colin but he was much more used to these competitions, and didn't spot how badly I was affected by the occasion. I remember feeling completely lost and alone on the morning of the final. I didn't know how to cope. I was suddenly very nervous and couldn't control my feelings. Jennifer Stoute, the British sprinter, tried to keep me calm and make me feel more comfortable but I couldn't settle my nerves. Suddenly, it hit me that everyone was expecting me to win and I couldn't deal with it in my usual way. The comfort zone of my life and childhood had disappeared and I felt completely out of my depth. I knew how to win the race but I felt too sick to eat and drained by all the pressure that was on me.

I went to warm up on my own and the only other person there was the German athlete Grit Breuer. She was warming up with her coach and this made me feel even more alone. Colin, my coach and mentor, had to prepare for his own performance in the 60 metres hurdles so I couldn't go to him for advice. I tried hard to get myself motivated but I was scared and, even though I knew I had the ability to win, my mind took over. I wanted someone to help me out of this feeling but there was no one who could. Now I know that it was up to me to give myself the support, and find strength within myself to win. But at that time, I couldn't help myself. The weather was cold and grey and it felt like my mood. I wasn't confident about even walking into the stadium. I didn't feel good about anything.

The race started and the first 200 metres of the race was fine as I went through in 21.30 seconds. But on the back straight of the second lap, I felt my hamstring tugging and I was passed by Sunday Bada from Nigeria. He went on to beat me by about a tenth of a second and took the gold. I can remember thinking that he had just won the race I needed to have won. That tenth of a second was enormous to me. Yes, I had got a silver medal but on the winners' rostrum all I could think was that I had failed and let everyone down. It was the best medal I had won indoors, but it wasn't what I was expected to get and second best just wasn't good enough. Meeting my mum and dad and girlfriend and family afterwards was terrible. No one knew what to say to me. It was the most awful feeling and in the post-race interviews I could see that the interviewers were disappointed too. I hated the question from the reporters, 'How do you feel?' I felt dreadful—what else could I say to them?

I flew home on the same flight as Colin that evening and went back to the flat alone. Susannah and Jay were still in Paris as I had come home on the athletes' flight. I sat looking at my silver medal, knowing that the outside world was carrying on as usual; but my world was still. Without my family to talk to it was so much worse. It was a huge lesson to me about life. All I could think was that I was alone in Cwmbrân, I was a devastated World Indoors Silver medallist, but life was going on around me despite how I was feeling. I had a really tough time being on my own that evening. I realised that the world didn't revolve around me and winning medals. It put my life and sport into perspective and, once again, showed me how much I relied on others. Perhaps that was the lesson for me. I was expected to win and what I learned was that you have to get your strength from within and not rely on anyone else. I wasn't ready to cope with the title of World Champion and needed support.

Never again. Next time I went out I knew that I had trained hard, I believed in myself and I was in charge of my destiny. Next time I knew how to prepare and I knew even more how to rely on myself. The hard thing for me had been the questioning of myself. Next time I went for a title, there was no question.

CHAPTER SEVEN

TURNING SILVER INTO GOLD

The year 1997 improved, however. The World Championships in Athens meant our relay team would be back together. I was now coached by Linford Christie. He was a brilliant coach and I enjoyed my time with him. I still get on very well with him. He was great at motivating his athletes before any race. In this year, he took all of us—Katherine, Darren, Paul and me—into a room and told us to listen to the lyrics on the track he was about to play for us. He said, 'I could give you a speech but I won't . . . listen to this.' He then put on R Kelly's 'I believe I can fly'. All of us listened with huge lumps in our throats and we struggled to look at each other. The words were perfect for the goal we had been set.

We were very emotional and the track became the one I used to play time and time again to set me up for my races.

I also competed in the World Championship 400 metres individual event, and actually beat the great Michael Johnson in the heats to make it to the final. Sadly, though, the pressure got to me and I came eighth in the final, so I knew I had something to make up in the relay. The team was the same four members as for the Olympics but the order had changed. Selecting the running order for a relay is all about team tactics and playing to individuals' strengths. The first leg runner must have control and be able to run at an even pace. To run the second leg, you need to be aware of your surroundings and have a fast turnover to get the team set up. The job of the third leg runner is to hold the position and to be a consistent runner that the others can rely on. Finally, the fourth leg runner, or anchorman, has to be very courageous and strong under pressure.

I was now on third leg and would be following Roger Black. Iwan Thomas had a great first leg and Roger faced the American Antonio Pettigrew, who ran an amazingly fast race. When I got the baton, we were in third position and quite far back, with America and Jamaica ahead. I knew I had to give Mark Richardson a chance and I went off, catching up and overtaking the American and in the process making up a huge deficit. In the home straight, the American passed me but even then we were only a couple of metres behind as I handed over the baton. Mark ended up a close second and I think that was one of the best relay legs of my career because I made up such a lot of ground in a World Championship final.

The crowd had gone wild as I

spurted ahead in the back straight. David Coleman, commentating for the BBC, had said during the race, 'Wait Jamie! Wait! Don't go!' which I felt was oddly negative. I'd run my heart out and tried to do the utmost for my team in the best way I knew how. We were all bitter at coming second again and hugely disappointed, and our celebrations after the race didn't have the same feel as at the Olympics the year before. But the Americans were just so strong, and, in the end, we had done well to get the silver. Adrian Thomas and Steve Perks, two Welshmen, were great relay coaches who we had had huge respect for and our medal was as much for them as it was for us.

Sadly, in 2007 came news that Antonio Pettigrew from the victorious American team had admitted to using banned substances to aid his performance. We all felt cheated because we had spent so many years disappointed with our performance at not gaining the gold. We were upgraded, but the gold medal was a tarnished one as we had lost out on the ceremony and hearing the anthem play for us. We campaigned to receive our medals as a team so that we might enjoy the success that was denied to us in 1997. As it turned out, however, Iwan and I were given our medals at the National Assembly's Senedd building in Cardiff. We didn't even get the original medals or replicas of them, which was bitterly disappointing and lessened their worth in our eyes. We would have liked to have been presented with the medals at a major athletics meet to show that we were being recognised as a team for our achievement. When you compete as an athlete, you compete to win and winning like this is very sad. However, the real sadness in all of this is that Antonio Pettigrew committed suicide in 2010, leaving behind a wife and son. That to me is the real tragedy from all of this. Sport is not worth cheating for. To win is great but not at any price.

I can honestly say that I trained really hard to be the best I could and to make my parents proud of me. I worked hard for my family, my children, my friends and for everyone who came to watch me. I never really ran for the money but I always ran for the medals, even as I became more successful. As a boy, my parents used to take me to the local running tracks to what were called 'Medal Meetings' and for winning at those I got my medal and my steak!

I can look at my medals and feel proud of what I've achieved. But being deprived of a medal because of someone else's cheating is a bitter pill to swallow.

*   *   *

In 1998 we won the European Championships 400 metres relay in Hungary. This time I was sharing with Iwan. He was an absolute genius on the track but a bag of nerves and not at all positive before he went out to compete. 1998 was his year but he was still like a frightened rabbit and it was up to me to give him the reassurance he needed.

Then we trained together in South Africa in preparation for the World Cup, and we raced against each other at the Commonwealth Games in Kuala Lumpur, where we had time to talk to each other on the track as we ran together. However, in the final, just as the starter was about to call us to our marks, I realised I had a very expensive Tag Heuer watch on and that I couldn't run wearing it. I threw it to someone in the crowd and could only remember that the man had grey hair and a yellow coat. It was all I could think about during the race and at 200 metres in I suddenly realised I was in a race and had to get my mind on the job. I totally ruined my race because of a watch!

Remembering my disappointment at the World Indoor Championships in Paris two years earlier, I knew I had to put things right at the World Indoor Championships in 1999 in Maebashi, Japan. I'd be running as an individual there. I went to Australia to train and came fourth in a small race and felt completely devastated. I panicked and felt like I had in Paris.

Then I went to train with the legendary sprinter Frankie Fredericks, from Namibia. He ran with me and built my confidence without either of us realising quite how much. He was a stunning sprinter but I was able to keep up with him and I knew then that he was giving me the confidence I needed ahead of the race. I was thrilled to be able to keep up with such a sprinting icon over 200 metres. I even told my good friend Darren Campbell before the race that I would use my 400 metres winner's money to pay for a top-notch meal for us and the rest of the team.

My confidence was high and at the warm-up track I didn't let the situation get the better of me. I could see the other competitors warming up, doing their drills, and I refused to let them intimidate me. I stood my ground and my confidence got to them; they moved aside to let me complete my drills. I really wanted to win. Out on the track I can remember thinking *Relax*, until near the end when I kicked away from the rest of the field and I crossed the line as World Champion. I had destroyed the demons that were in my head and got rid of the awful memories of Paris.

I ran to phone my dad from the track and said, 'Dad! Your son is World Champion!' He burst out crying and that, for me, was the best prize ever. To make my father proud was like being in my own *Rocky* movie. I was alone in Japan but this time I didn't need anyone supporting me because I'd got my confidence from within. I have a great deal to thank Frankie Fredericks for because his training sessions gave me the boost I really needed. Athletics is 90% belief. You can have talent but unless you believe strongly in yourself you'll never win.

*   *   *

A combination of things led to my retirement from the sport even though I was running well. I got injured and realised how much I was missing my family. My second son, Morgan, was born in 2003 and saying goodbye to the boys and Susannah, to be away for long periods of time, got harder and harder. To be a successful athlete you have to be selfish and put yourself first. I had three people at home who I really wanted to be with and who were first in my eyes. Susannah was finding it difficult that as a family we were apart for such long periods and I phoned my coach at the time, Innocent Egbunike, and told him that I needed to go home. He was a wonderful coach and a wonderful friend, and saying goodbye was very emotional. His saying to me whenever we trained was 'Speak the truth and shame the devil.' I had to tell the truth and I had to go home. People have asked me if I have regretted it but I had a great time in sport, and all the wonderful things that I have been able to do since because of my sport make it all worthwhile.

CHAPTER EIGHT

HEROES

Athletics has given me an awful lot. I have made great friends in the sport and although we don't see each other regularly, we are all in touch. Fellow athletes from home and competitors from around the globe have been an important part of my career. I've been lucky enough to meet some of my heroes, too, and I know how important those people have been for me. I used to love watching the American sprinter and long jumper Carl Lewis. To me he was an absolute legend, with his ten Olympic medals, nine of which were gold. I met him at the Olympics in 1996 and I had my photo taken with him and that made me really proud. Now he's a friend of mine on Facebook! We don't chat but we are linked and this is amazing to me.

I loved Daley Thompson, the decathlon double Olympic gold medallist, too. He was a hero in Britain when I was growing up. He took the sport to a new level because he wasn't just a sports star, he was a hero. Everyone loved him. He was outspoken, he was funny and he was a winner. We all thought he was a huge character but he was also committed and totally believed in himself. He knew he would win. He even trained on Christmas Day! As a youngster I saw him competing and wanted to be as good as that. He made the Adidas brand cool. Recently, I did some work with him for BBC Sport Relief and we exchanged mobile numbers and we keep in touch. When he phones, I still think: That's Daley Thompson— *the* Daley Thompson!

Colin Jackson and Linford Christie are two other heroes in athletics but to me they're my mates as well, and

I'm proud to call them that.

The 400 metres is my event and the ultimate 400 metres runner for me is the great Michael Johnson. Michael's speed is phenomenal. I've raced him several times. His ability is incredible and he has inspired me because of his talent and achievements. He has a huge aura and wherever he goes, people stop to give him respect. Even when he was warming up at the track, all the other athletes would stop to watch him, even those competing in field events. He has always been one of athletics' key figures and continues to inspire younger athletes who long to emulate his achievements.

Gareth Edwards was my dad's hero. I used to watch my dad on International rugby days sitting on the living room floor with his hands in the air shouting at the Welsh rugby team on the television, 'Come on! Come on!' I have wonderful memories of seeing him screaming with joy as his hero scored. Years later I was with Gareth on an evening out and remember looking at him and thinking: That is Gareth Edwards and he is a legend and my dad's hero. I had to phone my dad to tell him who I was with and I asked Gareth to speak to him. I was so proud that after all my dad had done for me, I could make his day too! I know my dad went to the rugby club the next day to tell everyone who he had spoken to. Heroes are important to us all.

*   *   *

I went with Colin Jackson to the Brit awards in 1997. Colin and Vinnie Jones were giving an award to the Manic Street Preachers. I dressed for the event in Armani and D&G, and everyone said I looked the business. All the celebrities of the time had been invited and our table included Louise Redknapp. Even Mrs Merton was there! Suddenly, across the room, I saw Lauryn Hill, the singer from the Fugees. I was a massive fan and Colin, Linford and I had seen them perform in concert in Australia a month before. I couldn't believe she was in the same room as me and, like a schoolboy, pointed her out to Colin. Colin was much more used to show business events than I was and his reaction was less excitable. He suggested we go over to meet her and I followed like a lapdog. Colin introduced himself to Wyclef Jean who was with Lauryn. She looked annoyed at being interrupted but then she turned to me and exclaimed, 'You're the 400 metres runner!' I couldn't speak. All I could think of was that she knew who I was! She started talking to me about how much she had loved track and field when she was in school and her favourite distance was 400 metres. I couldn't believe it! She knew my races but, more importantly, she knew who I was! It was one of the best moments in my life.

Later on, Colin went off to present his award and I ended up backstage with the legend Sir Tim Rice. I looked at the television backstage which was screening the event and couldn't believe it as Prince came up on stage. Sir Tim Rice had to reassure me it was live—I thought it must be an old programme showing! Two of my heroes in one evening was just too much! I had always had posters of Prince all over my walls. I went outside to wait next to the ramp near the stage and he walked past me, surrounded by huge bodyguards. Like a king, they put a long black coat around his shoulders which he shrugged off regally. He put his guitar down and we stood feet apart from each other. He looked at me. I opened my mouth to try to speak but the words just wouldn't come out. I was totally star-struck and he went off somewhere else. I immediately phoned up Susannah, leaving a message on her answer machine that made no sense. I could have kicked myself for not finding the voice to say anything to him at all.

As an athlete, I was an entertainer and loved showing off to the crowd. When I retired I wanted to feel the same buzz. Athletes are modern day entertainers, strutting and parading before their races, especially the sprinters. It was natural that I would do some television work. I was part of a television show called *Energize* and I found myself having to learn new skills to become a host for the show. It was a sports programme for young people and each week I tested a new sport with them and brought on champions like Dennis Bergkamp, the footballer, to talk about their sport. I also appeared on *A Question of Sport* on a regular basis and *They Think It's All Over*.

Appearing on *The Big Breakfast* with Denise van Outen was great fun! I had to be interviewed on the bed, which was quite convenient as I had been out late the night before, and thought it a good idea to get forty winks before filming. Suddenly the light came on to say we were live and she began asking me questions about my athletics and I was still half asleep! I also competed in *Superstars* for BBC1 and came third, so I'm very proud of that when you see the other athletes who took part, such as Sir Chris Hoy, Amir Khan, Alan Baxter, and of course, Colin Jackson. I keep having to test myself as I feel challenges are important and I've never been one to take the safe route. I also took part in a reality programme on BBC2, *Safari School*, where I joined a game reserve and learnt how to become a ranger alongside other celebrities from *Holby City*, *Neighbours* and *Bad Girls*. The school was on the Shamwari game reserve in South Africa and the challenge was to survive out in the bush using the skills we had been taught. There were some scary moments when I wished I was back on the track. Once, we were cut off by a herd of elephants who wanted to stampede us. The secret we had been taught in the bush is never to run. We all moved briskly which became a jog and finally a run and on camera you can see the fear on our faces as we made it to the jeep just in time. In another incident, we realised the difference between meeting lions in the zoo and being placed in their territory and their environment. Again, we knew not to turn away from a lion's gaze, but it was very hard as they caught sight of us and started walking slowly towards us. I suddenly felt serious fear, being close to such a powerful animal with such presence. My claim to fame during the competition was that we had to make a fire and cook venison for a well-known chef from South Africa. I cooked for the boys' team and our meat won for the best flavours. I knew my mum would be really proud of me for that!

Another challenge was taking part in *Cirque de Celebrité* on Sky television when I learnt to become a circus act. Again, I was competing against a range of other celebrities like the model Emma B, Kenzie from Blazin' Squad and Mark Bright, the footballer. Each week we were live and learning a new circus art. It was extremely scary, even more so when I learnt that in the first week Simon Cowell was in the audience looking up at me!

I had to juggle and spin and move acrobatically, on top of a large ball. We were taught by Carmen who was a very hard taskmaster but when you got something right she was quick to offer praise. I really practised because I knew from my days in sport that only practice makes perfect. One stunt I had to do was on a trapeze, high up in the air. Shortly into the routine, I got into difficulties and I wasn't able to follow the procedure they had taught me. I wasn't able to kick wide enough and suddenly I could feel the trapeze giving way and I was hurtling to the floor. There was no safety net, just one man beneath holding a safety rope which took my weight. As the rope spun through his hands it finally became taut about a metre from the ground. I had fallen from a huge height and it completely unnerved me! I got a sense of just how dangerous circus acts are. The life may be exciting but it wasn't for me. I was glad to come out in one piece. I have huge respect for anyone who works with circus arts. They have the balance and grace of some of the greatest athletes in the world and they put as much effort into their training, too.

Even though I have retired from professional sport, I still can't leave sport totally. I was invited by Steve

McNamara, Head Coach of the Bradford Bulls rugby league team, to work with them as a sprinting coach to improve their speed training, and enjoyed being part of a very different environment. I met with them at Odsal Stadium in Bradford and was genuinely excited to be given the chance to work using my skills in a different field. I gave motivational talks and mini-sprint sessions and they seemed to really welcome working in this way as a change.

I also enjoy coaching football projects, helping promising young footballers with their sprinting skills. I have worked with players from a number of different clubs from Cardiff City to Manchester City and I love seeing the difference I can make. Youngsters respond so well to trying something new. I tell them in my first session that starting a sprint is like a pilot about to take off. The trick is to keep low so that you always have a smooth take off and don't jerk as you go into full speed. It's surprising how effective little stories like this can be in getting a message across. It's often the simple things that stick in the mind longest, and can really make a difference.

CHAPTER NINE

BLISTER MISTER

Sport has been too much a part of my life for me to turn my back on it. When I retired, I started to work in the field of sports management but not in the usual way. I used my art skills from my school and college days and established a new style rugby calendar with the Welsh Rugby Union which enjoyed record sales. This led to further design consultancy work with them for the Six Nations programme covers. In 2006, I was asked to become the team attaché for the Wales Commonwealth Games team. I acted as a representative for Wales and felt incredibly proud to be given such an honour. As part of my role, I put together the team kit, to ensure that they not only felt like a team, but looked like a team as well. I brought in a designer clothing label team to make suits and organised everything, even down to the hair products!

I attended numerous functions and the highlight was to be given the task of making Welsh cakes for a large group of Australians in Melbourne at a food festival for the Games. I had to talk as I cooked—the talking wasn't difficult, but following the recipe book at the same time was! I'd never cooked Welsh cakes before but a quick call to my mum back at home had put me on the right track.

I now manage Definitive Sports, a sports management company involved with current key athletes such as Wales and Ospreys rugby player Shane Williams, Olympic bronze medallist Tasha Danvers, 11-time Paralympic gold medallist Dave Roberts, the British, European and Commonwealth Champion hurdler Dai Greene and many more. I also enjoy working as a director of Superschools, an organisation which gets Olympic athletes into schools to exercise with kids and encourages them to participate in sport while raising their awareness of a healthy and active lifestyle. I see in the kids the same enthusiasm I had for sport at their age. I'm a consultant to the Jaguar Academy of Sport which features great sporting names like the cricketer Sir Ian Botham, and athletes such as Dame Kelly Holmes and Denise Lewis. I try to use the skills I learnt from my sport in my new career in business. The same ethics apply as far as I am concerned—train hard, work hard, focus on the job and get the result.

Many of these principles are included in the BBC's project *Raise your Game* and it's great for me to be an ambassador for this, linking up again with my ex-mentor Colin Jackson who leads the project. There are no short cuts in life, as in sport. You won't succeed on the track if you're lazy and it's the same in life. In sport, you have to take risks but you have prepared your body well to do this. In business, if you prepare properly, the results will come. My years as part of a relay team have meant that I am used to working with and respecting others. As the great coaches always say: 'There is no "I" in team.'

Recently, I was awarded an honorary fellowship by the University of Wales to mark my commitment to the people and community of south-east Wales. I consider it an amazing honour to be given the same award as Lord Kinnock and Sir Terry Matthews and I'm immensely proud that my family were able to share in this special day. Taking part in the awards ceremony, I realised how impressive it is to be a student and collect your reward for years of study. I didn't go to university but I said in my speech how important it was to me to be recognised for my years of commitment and hard work in the world of athletic competition. I made everyone laugh when I gave my speech but I ended by saying that the degree really belonged to my mum and dad, my girlfriend and my two sons because of all that they have done for me to help make this happen.

I still love to train regularly and still set myself goals to achieve. In 2010 I was asked, as an Olympic athlete, to race against a horse at Kempton Park racecourse over 100 metres, earning £10,000 for charity. This was the first race of its kind and although Peopleton Brook, the race horse, certainly beat me, I loved doing it for Barnado's Cymru and since then I have been made an official ambassador for the charity. This event gave me great personal satisfaction. It's a way of raising money for a good cause and I'm one of the few who is mad enough to accept the challenge!

I love athletics. To make a living out of something you love doing is very special. I wish the same for my sons so that they can feel as fulfilled and be as happy as I have been. My sons are free to do whatever they want to do and I want them to have choice. Both have their mum's talent for drama and both have made starts at their own acting careers. I will be proud of them whatever they do. I just want them to be happy, and to be the best dad for them. They know that I will be there to support and encourage them to be the best they can be. I have learnt in my career that it pays to respect others and to give your best. And it's important to look for opportunities to showcase what you have, rather than worrying about what everyone else has.

Probably the biggest lesson that I have learnt from sport is how to take defeat graciously and how to be humble when you are successful.

But I have always believed that whatever you do, either in sport or in life, you should do it with a smile on your face. If you enjoy something you will make more of an effort to do it to the best of your ability. Always be yourself no matter how much pressure you get from those around you. A good friend of mine said to me, 'You're your own sun.' I asked her what she meant and she said that I didn't need a sun to make myself shine. I took that as the most wonderful compliment. I have always tried to share my positive attitude with those around me.

The gym for me now is a social place rather than my workplace. My competitive spirit isn't quite lost though, as I have committed myself to enter for the London Marathon. My challenge is to beat Iwan Thomas. The old rivalry is still there between two Welshmen. My father used to say to me when I went out to compete: 'Blister mister', meaning *give it all you've got*. I hope I have done that and will continue to live life to the maximum. I may not run any more, but I'll never slow down.

FRANCESCA SIMON

FELAKET HENRY'NİN İNTİKAMI

FRANCESCA SIMON Yale ve Oxford Üniversiteleri'nde eğitim gördükten sonra serbest gazeteci olarak çalıştı. Halen başarılı bir çocuk kitabı yazarı olarak, kocası ve oğlu Joshua ile birlikte Londra'da yaşıyor.

Horrid Henry's Revenge

© 2001 Francesca Simon (text copyright)

© 2001 Tony Ross (illustration copyright)

2001'de The Orion Publishing Group Ltd Orion House'un yan kuruluşu olan Orion Children's Book (Londra) tarafından yayımlanmıştır.

Onk Ajans Ltd.

İletişim Yayınları 1054 • Çocuk Kitapları Dizisi 12
ISBN 975-05-0305-8
© 2005 İletişim Yayıncılık A. Ş.
1. BASKI 2005, İstanbul (1000 adet)
2. BASKI 2005, İstanbul (1000 adet)
3. BASKI 2006, İstanbul (1000 adet)

EDİTÖR Bahar Siber
KAPAK Suat Aysu
KAPAK FİLMİ 4 Nokta Grafik
UYGULAMA Hüsnü Abbas
DÜZELTİ Bahri Özcan
MONTAJ Şahin Eyilmez
BASKI ve CİLT Sena Ofset

İletişim Yayınları
Binbirdirek Meydanı Sokak İletişim Han No. 7 Cağaloğlu 34122 İstanbul
Tel: 212.516 22 60-61-62 • Faks: 212.516 12 58
e-mail: iletisim@iletisim.com.tr • web: www.iletisim.com.tr